Art of Psychotherapy

A Clinical Psychologist's Guide

ANN GAMSA, PH.D.

 FriesenPress

One Printers Way
Altona, MB R0G 0B0
Canada

www.friesenpress.com

Copyright © 2024 by Ann Gamsa, Ph.D.
First Edition — 2024

ISBN
978-1-03-831141-2 (Hardcover)
978-1-03-831140-5 (Paperback)
978-1-03-831142-9 (eBook)

1. PSYCHOLOGY, PSYCHOTHERAPY

Distributed to the trade by The Ingram Book Company

Table of Contents

1.
Introduction

The fabric of this guide for psychotherapists is woven from my many years in psychotherapy practice, from my time as Director of Psychological Services in a hospital multidisciplinary pain centre, and from the invaluable lessons I have learned from clients, trainees, and colleagues.

The Art of Psychotherapy argues that a comprehensive examination and treatment of mental health problems cannot be contained within the confines of a behavioural science. Early in my practice as a clinical psychologist, I learned that the person sitting in front of me did not conform to scientific expectations. Rather, my clients demonstrated that psychotherapy is an art, involving the expression and communication of human emotions and thoughts in a variety of ways that do not follow the rigorous criteria of scientific methodology.

This guide introduces the new psychologist to optimal procedures for conducting successful psychotherapy, and helps psychologists already in practice to improve the outcome of their work with clients.

The guide begins with a definition of psychotherapy and a brief review of its history, followed by an examination of psychotherapy as a discipline conforming to the domain of art more than to that

1

of science. Next comes an example of the first few sessions in psychotherapy,, followed by a section on questions I continue to ponder about the psychotherapy process—questions that do not lend themselves to straightforward, unambiguous answers.

From there, we examine the common factors across different theoretical approaches in psychology, followed by a discussion of *therapeutic alliance* between client and psychotherapist.

An examination of how defences are triggered when a person feels emotionally threatened, is followed by a discussion of how important it is for therapists to use non-technical language to ensure effective communication.

For optimal overall therapeutic benefit, a recommendation is made for psychologists to work with their clients on *recurring themes* underlying the problems presented rather than on solving specific problems.

Towards the end of this guide, the different theoretical approaches currently employed in psychotherapy are reviewed. The guide ends with a summary description of the effective clinical psychologist, including knowledge, skills, and personal characteristics.

I hope the reader will take away from this guide the many lessons I have learned from my clients and colleagues, lessons which have vastly improved my work as a clinical psychologist.

The appendices provide the reader with an example of an initial assessment report, followed by a form for clients to list the goals they wish to attain with the help of psychotherapy. The final appendix provides a list of metaphors whose use can enhance therapy interventions. Case examples are presented throughout the guide, some from my own practice. Names and other identifying features have been changed to protect confidentiality.

2.
Some Words to the Neophyte Psychologist

While you can expect the work ahead of you to be enriching and deeply gratifying, it will also be challenging and occasionally, frustrating. Each person seeking your help comes with a unique story embedded in their personal world; no two will be alike. Be prepared for the gratification of nurturing joy in someone who previously knew only misery. Know that, despite your best efforts, some clients you will not be able to help. All this is inherent in the profession you have chosen.

You have worked long and hard to earn the honorific, "PhD in Psychology". On completing your oral defence, you are congratulated and celebrated by your supervisors, other professors, family, and friends. You breathe a sigh of relief. You've "arrived"! You are now a full-fledged, accredited psychologist ready to ply your knowledge in the service of individuals suffering from mental health problems. Your job is to help them live, work, love, and play with ease and enjoyment.

Before seeing your first client, with your framed doctoral certificate displayed on the wall, reflect on the immense power and responsibility you now hold as you minister to fragile souls. While psychotherapy is an honoured and honourable enterprise, it is no simple task.

Your studies have equipped you with theories and evidence-based techniques founded on methodologically sound research and statistical analysis. In university graduate programs, psychotherapy is often taught within the framework of one or more theoretical approaches—recipes to be followed, built on science of the social genre. Certainly, the sanctified teachings are important, but do not mistake theory, technique, and scientific method for the core of psychotherapy. The essence of psychotherapy is to relieve suffering and foster well-being in the individual sitting with you in your office.

The central work of psychotherapy is not about adhering to a set of theoretical principles any more than the sciences of neuroanatomy, physiology, genetics, or cellular biology will help you truly understand the inner lived experience of your client. To do your job well, you will need to develop a deep and thorough understanding of each client's unique, multilayered lived experience.

Learnings
- Psychotherapists must use their power with care and responsibility—always in the interest of the client's well-being.
- A deep understanding of the multifaceted, multilayered, unique individual client fosters healing in psychotherapy.
- The psychotherapist's job is to help clients live, work, love, and play with ease and enjoyment.

3.
Defining Psychotherapy

Casting a broad net, psychotherapy entails some form of communication between a person seeking help for mental health problems and a "healer" who works to lessen suffering and enhance the seeker's well-being. In current professional parlance, psychotherapy involves a professional relationship between a patient/client and a psychotherapist who uses validated therapeutic principles, procedures, and techniques consonant with the local culture, to improve the person's mental health and well-being.

According to the American Psychological Association (2017):

> "Psychotherapy involves communication between a client and a therapist, and is intended to help people:
> - Find relief from emotional distress;
> - Seek solutions to problems in their lives, such as dealing with disappointment, grief, family problems, and job or career dissatisfaction;
> - Modify ways of thinking and acting that are preventing them from working productively and enjoying personal relationships."

According to the Order of Psychologists of Quebec in Canada, psychotherapy is understood to "encompass psychological treatment for a mental health disorder, behavioural disturbance, or other problem resulting in psychological suffering or distress, and has as its purpose to foster significant changes in the client's cognitive, emotional, or behavioural functioning, interpersonal relations, personality, or health" (l'Institut national d'excellence en santé et en services sociaux, 2018, p. 10).

Noteworthy in this definition is the inclusion of physical health within a psychologist's domain of practice. An abundance of research shows that psychological strategies such as visualization and relaxation exercises, as well as expectation effects, can have important impact on the immune system and other determinants of health (Marchant, 2016). We may thus extend the definition of psychotherapy to include treatment of certain physical health problems in addition to those of mental health.

An example of how psychotherapy can successfully treat physical problems is illustrated by one of my past clients, whom I'll call Debra.

Case Study: Debra

Debra, a 30-year-old administrative assistant, came to see me for help with poor sleep, daytime fatigue, headaches, and dizziness. While she had been fully worked up by a neurologist, test results did not show any disease process. Debra was very anxious about succeeding in her job and feared she might be fired for not being good enough. While discussing her competence level, it became abundantly clear that she was highly skilled in the tasks required in her current job. She had been let go from her previous work because she did not have adequate experience to succeed in that job. Her current anxiety threatened her confidence level, and in turn, her competence.

Having established that her knowledge was fully adequate for her current job, we worked on increasing Debra's feeling of competence, and thus her confidence. I also taught her deep breathing exercises to help her relax and sleep more easily at night. Debra was fully compliant, using the deep breathing a few times a day, and at night when she got into bed. She soon began to fall asleep without difficulty and was able to get back to sleep quickly after waking a couple of times during the night. I also encouraged her to do cardio exercise several times a week. After six months of therapy, she no longer felt fatigued during the day, the headaches had abated, and the dizziness disappeared. Her boss had also complimented her several times for the quality of her work.

Psychotherapeutic strategies had clearly helped to alleviate the broad range of physical symptoms for which Debra sought help.

Learnings
- Psychotherapy involves some form of communication between a person seeking help for mental health problems and a healer who works to help the seeker.
- Healers usually use methods consistent with the belief system of their culture.
- Symptoms such as panic attacks that manifest themselves both emotionally and physically can be helped by means of psychological interventions.

4.
Psychotherapy: A Brief Historical View

According to Jerome Frank (1974), all cultures possess healers who assume the role of "psychotherapist" by applying some form of ritual consonant with the culture's belief system to improve a person's well-being. In some cultures, the shaman plays this role; in others, the role is played by a psychiatrist or psychologist. Regardless of the specific method used, the healer is expected to have certain healing powers that others in the community do not possess. The shaman works in a culture with a "religio-magical" healing tradition, while the trained Western psychotherapist is expected to utilize treatment based on a theory with scientific underpinnings. Frank defines psychotherapy as a "healing relationship using socially authorized methods in a series of contacts primarily involving words, acts, and rituals regarded as forms of persuasion and rhetoric" (Reisner, 2005, p.377). In this definition, psychotherapy, in one form or another, has existed for as long as we have written records.

A historical and cross-cultural examination of records from as far back as 1500 BC reveals a myriad of treatment approaches used to help individuals with mental health problems. Included are approaches as diverse as shamanism, Vedic healing, and religious and magical practices. Certainly, the teachings of Jesus seem to have been aimed at calming anxiety in his followers. For many, they continue to do so today. "Cast all your anxiety on him because he cares for you" (*New King James Bible*, Peter 5:7).

Treatment approaches for the mentally ill are described by medieval Islamic thinkers such as Rhazes, Avicenna, and the poet Rumi. In the following poem, Rumi (1207–1273) offers a method for coping with difficult emotions and overcoming distress. Specifically, the poem suggests approaches much like the currently popular Mindfulness and Acceptance and Commitment Therapy (ACT), both of which centre on accepting and facing with equanimity, whatever life brings, whether it be joy or pain.

The Guest House

This being human is a guest house.
Every morning a new arrival.
A joy, a depression, a meanness,
some momentary awareness comes
as an unexpected visitor.
Welcome and entertain them all!
Even if they are a crowd of sorrows,
who violently sweep your house
empty of its furniture,
still, treat each guest honorably.
He may be clearing you out
for some new delight.
The dark thought, the shame, the malice,
meet them at the door laughing and invite them in.
Be grateful for whatever comes,
because each has been sent
as a guide from beyond. (Al-Din Rumi, 2008, p. 588)

We can date the beginning of our currently recognized Western forms of psychotherapy from about 1886, when Sigmund Freud began his private psychoanalytic practice in Vienna (Evan, 2023). Since that time to the present, many different models of psychotherapy have been introduced, developed, applied clinically, and researched. They can be grouped into several broad categories, including psychoanalytic, cognitive, behavioural, cognitive-behavioural, existential-humanistic, and integrative therapies. These models will be described in some detail later in this guide.

<u>Learnings</u>
- All cultures have institutionalized approaches to help people with mental health problems.
- A culture's approaches to treatment of mental illness fits with the cultural view of mediators of illness and health.

5.
Psychotherapy: Science or Art?

We live in a scientific age. Psychotherapy treatments are accepted by academia, professional organizations, and insurance companies only when they are "evidence based," i.e., validated by published, methodologically sound research and statistical analysis; standardized formulations; and approved therapy techniques. Clinical psychologists are sometimes referred to as "science practitioners," and the discipline has long been regarded as a "behavioural science" (Wolman, 1989).

Young and Heller (2000) argue persuasively that, while psychotherapy may be informed by science, the practice itself cannot be rigorously scientific. Furthermore, research has shown "that rigid adherence to a protocol can attenuate the alliance and increase resistance to the treatment" (Wampold & Imel, 2015, p.275), while treatment tailored to the individual client's needs produces better outcomes (Wampold & Imel, 2015). Furthermore, the individual characteristics of the client and the therapist, as well as the complex interaction between the two, are critically important to the therapy process and outcome. These multiple variables do not lend themselves easily to rigorous scientific formulations.

Noteworthy are the changing definitions and descriptions of mental illnesses in sequential editions of the *Diagnostic and*

Statistical Manual of Mental Disorders (DSM), reflecting changes in sociocultural norms over time (McHenry, 2022). For example, early editions of the DSM classified homosexuality as a "mental illness" (Drescher, 2015). In 1973, the members attending a convention of the American Psychiatric Association (APA) voted to remove homosexuality from the list of mental disorders, and instead, adopted the term "sexual orientation disturbance." In 1987, homosexuality was completely removed from the DSM. Diagnostic changes based on voting, with changes over time, can hardly be considered "scientific."

While we can analyze the light spectrum in a sunset, the mechanisms of transmission between retina and brain, areas of brain activation, as well as correlations between brain activation and a person's report of their experience, none of these measurable *scientific* data tell us anything about the individual's lived experience of the sunset. Nor can auditory data convey the feeling of joy inspired by Beethoven's Ninth Symphony or the sadness evoked by parts of his late quartets.

Use of a *scientific*, evidence-based method with results derived from statistical analysis may provide a useful *norm*. However, statistically based results are not applicable to all—or even most—individuals. In fact, the results for individuals in published studies typically get lost in statistically based conclusions.

There is no doubt that science expands, enriches, and adds precision to our knowledge, but it can tell us little about the inner lived experience of the person undergoing therapy. Nor can the numerical data determine how the therapist might best respond to the person's emotional reactions and needs. Young and Heller write: "Science is not really capable of creating instruments that can detect the full range of signals that a human organism can react to. The human organism can detect miniscule inflections in facial, non-verbal, and emotional signals, minute details of behavior, their possible meaning, and their place in a given context..." (2000, p. 129).

This is where the art enters. While conducting psychotherapy, employ the theories, techniques, and basic principles as laid out in the textbooks of psychotherapy, but use these only as a framework to uphold your creative, dynamic, relational "art." To the well-learned tools and techniques, add empathy, sensitivity, and deep understanding of the person in front of you.

As you listen to the client's narrative, enhance the encounter by displaying an open receptiveness together with carefully considered and optimally timed interventions. Observe and listen attentively to the reactions your interventions elicit; sometimes they will reveal complex layers of meaning, carrying important information for your understanding of the client and her problems. A psychologist who is *present* to a client's emotional reactions is engaging in the "art" of the therapeutic encounter.

The importance of being in the moment with a client is illustrated by the following example.

Case Study: James

James returned to therapy after 22 years, to get help in his marital relationship. His wife was accusing him of lying in many situations. In one example, she did not believe that his father had neglected him and had often strapped him when he was a child because now, in his old age, his father was kind and caring. I was able to acknowledge that I remembered from his therapy many years earlier that his father had been abusive.

This simple acknowledgement elicited the following response from James: "I feel so much better that you remember how things were for me. I was

> beginning to fear my memory had gone down
> the drain, and I was starting to believe my wife's
> accusation that I was making things up about my
> childhood just to get pity from her."

My full presence at the time of the encounter, and therefore my accurate recall of James' earlier years, made all the difference.

If you are so inclined, introduce humour, but only if you are certain your client will "get it" and share your amusement. When humour is delivered to the right person at the right time, the resulting mutual understanding can foster therapeutic alliance, a solid trusting relationship between therapist and client.

Every intervention must serve the therapy process, and aim ultimately to foster a beneficial outcome for the client. Over time—regardless of the theoretical approach used—the skilled therapist who listens attentively to the client's reactions, will anticipate how the client is likely to respond to a given intervention. There is no theory that will tell you how to do this.

Rather, your ability to synchronize your art with your client's emotional state flows from a deep and accurate overall under-standing of your client. When you have come to know your client well (personal history, interests, values, attitudes, emotional ten-dencies, and general knowledge), you can feel free to add relevant references involving poetry, visual art, religion, history, politics, or literature if you believe such interventions will advance this person's therapy.

When Sharon, a student in art history, described how frantically her mother screamed whenever Sharon disobeyed her, I said that her depiction reminded me of the painting, *The Scream* by Edvard Munch. Because I was certain Sharon was familiar with the paint-ing, I used this intervention to strengthen therapeutic alliance by referring to an image she could connect to her screaming mother.

Sharon smiled and became tearful at the same time, acknowledging her appreciation of the reference I had used.

Read widely: good fiction, history, politics, religion, poetry, and philosophy—read, read, read. The broader your knowledge of the world around you, the better you will be equipped to understand and help the diversity of clients who will come to you. Each one comes with a unique personal, historical, and cultural story. Coming to the encounter with knowledge pertaining to a given person's story promotes therapeutic alliance and facilitates beneficial therapy outcome. For example, knowing about a war in which the client's father was killed or about the basics of different religions allows you to better connect with the hurt or burden the client carries, and at the same time, increases the trust invested in you.

On the other hand, if you are not familiar with a topic your client raises, simply ask to be informed. It is no sin for you to expose a specific lack of knowledge. Furthermore, in explaining a subject to you, the client's own confidence may grow as a by-product of providing you with information.

The person sitting with you in your office is not a "conceptualization" or "diagnosis" seeking help via a "treatment model," but rather a complex, feeling, thinking, hurting individual who comes to you for relief from suffering and improvement in well-being. Get to know—really know—this person beyond the theoretical formulation of the "case." Understand what she feels and what moves, motivates, delights, and hurts her. Sometimes a single word from you—if it is just the right word, image, or metaphor—can become a powerful catalyst for healing and positive change. The gentlest touch of this person's core may loosen what's been locked in—the fears, fossilized memories, hurts, infelicitous thoughts, and habits of mind. With compassion, imagination, understanding, and skill, the psychotherapist can dare to become an inspired artist (and not only a theory-driven technician).

When you first learn a new ballroom dance, you practise the individual steps until they flow effortlessly. While you are still learning the individual steps, you are not yet "dancing." Similarly, if a therapist concentrates only on theory-based techniques (steps), he is not truly engaged with the client (partner) and may tread on the partner's "toes." The real dance begins only after the therapist has fully mastered the steps, integrated them into muscle memory, and is free to be fully engaged in the art of the therapy dance with the partner. He can now improvise, depart from the prescribed steps, and move with ease and poise in sync with the partner while gracefully leading the direction of the dance. This is the *art of psychotherapy.*

Sometimes, your therapeutic art may take you just outside standard psychotherapy practice. When your intervention breaches conventional methods, be clear about your rationale for using it. The case of Joan provides such an example.

Case Study: Joan

Joan, a devout Christian woman, suffered from severe, unremitting depression. From childhood, her church had been a second home; her family was deeply involved in the church community. She sang in the choir, and sometimes she led prayers. Six months earlier she had stopped going to church, ashamed to be seen so despondent by members of the congregation. She did not feel at all like the person they had come to know, admire, and love. At the same time, she felt guilty for her failure to rise above the depression. In some sense, she felt her inability to overcome depression was a betrayal of God. In the past, she had been a role model and mentor in the church, ministering to others in need.

Joan cried when she told me how much she missed singing in the choir. When I asked whether she sang hymns on her own at home, she said she felt unworthy to sing God's hymns. At this point I decided to take a risk and asked whether it would be okay for me to hum the melody of a hymn. With only a little hesitation, she agreed. I hummed "Jesus Loves Me," a hymn I was certain she knew. Before long, she was singing the words as I hummed, tears of comfort (as she later told me), streaming down her cheeks.

Initially, with Joan, there was no port of entry for questions, reason, or explanation—the typical tools for initiating psychotherapy. She was hurting too much for words. She needed a balm—much as a person parched with thirst needs water before they can speak. My humming of a well-known hymn opened the door to her comfort and trust, allowing her to begin to engage in the therapy that eventually relieved her suffering.

No scientific or theoretical approach provides instruction or technique for the therapist to hum a hymn. This is one example of the art of psychotherapy that I later entwined with a more standard Western psychotherapy approach that helped relieve Joan's crippling depression. After about 3 months of weekly therapy, she was able to return to church and again sing in the choir.

If you are just starting out, don't expect to become an artist overnight. First, you must practise the theoretical teachings and techniques you have been taught until their use feels effortless. Only when they are solidly integrated into your "muscle" memory can you free yourself from theory and prescribed interventions, depart from *the book*, and start to be an "artist." It takes time and experience to become fluid in your art, as well as imagination and courage to go beyond the accepted theoretical dictates and constraints of the day. In your first year of practice, seek supervision from an experienced psychologist you can trust. Be patient with yourself.

In summary, psychotherapy that employs a felicitous blend of science and art, tailored to the needs and experiences of the individual client, has been shown to ease distress and improve well-being (Hofmann & Weinberger, 2007). Science provides a model or framework, while art frees the therapist to minister to the needs of the unique individual.

Learnings
- While psychotherapy may be informed by science, it cannot conform to the rigorous requirements of scientific method.
- Definitions of certain diagnoses in the DSM have changed over time, as cultural views have changed.
- Only after fully grasping the scientific teachings of the practice of psychotherapy should the psychologist add "art" to the endeavour.
- Rigid adherence to theory or protocol can, in some cases, diminish the benefits of psychotherapy.
- The therapist with broad knowledge of the world about her (history, culture, religions, etc.) is best positioned to serve a diversity of clients.

6.

The First Few Sessions

The first psychotherapy session typically includes an assessment of the presenting problem or problems the client brings to therapy, together with a review of the client's overall psychosocial situation, past and present. This provides the therapist with the basic information for conducting therapy, sets up the relationship between client and therapist, and establishes the tone for the rest of the client's therapy.

A sample report reflecting the format of the initial assessment interview can be found in Appendix I. If the client's response to assessment questions does not follow the sequence as outlined in the Appendix report, there is no need to rigidly follow the order of topics as laid out there. Maintaining flexibility (rather than insisting on a predetermined structure) in this first session helps set the client at ease. At the same time, if the client digresses excessively, I may gently bring back the topic at hand. I also explain that, while I will be writing during the first session, I will also be listening attentively.

At the end of the first session, I reflect back to the client my understanding of the problem or problems she brings to therapy. I then ask whether I've understood correctly, as in the following example: "If I've understood correctly, you've experienced emotional and sexual abuse from boyfriends in the past. You've been forced by your parents to abort a pregnancy against your wishes, as well as the wishes of your current loving partner. You and he plan to marry. You don't want these experiences to negatively affect your current relationship or your future role as a mother. This is what you'd like help with in psychotherapy. Have I understood correctly, or is there something important I might have left out or misconstrued?"

In addition, I ask the client to let me know any time during the course of therapy, should she become aware that something I've said does not seem right or creates excessive unease. I acknowledge that, while I do my best, I don't always get it right. I also mention to clients that I will be honest with them; i.e., I will not flatter them falsely just to make them feel good. For example, I will not say to a client, "You're looking really good today," if I believe she's looking tired and bedraggled. Nor will I reassure her that she reacted optimally if I believe she was unnecessarily aggressive in a situation she describes.

All the above is to establish my style of conducting psychotherapy and to help the client feel comfortable with me and the therapy process. Before we come to the end of the first session, I ask whether the client has any questions for me. If I have learned the client has difficulty trusting or feels uneasy about being in therapy, I may ask whether she feels comfortable with me, emphasizing the need for an honest answer.

Typically, clients report feeling comfortable with me. Should a client say he is not at ease, we will explore the reason for this discomfort. Depending on the reason given, I will offer reassurance, encourage discussion of the client's discomfort, or possibly recommend another therapist more likely to suit the client's needs. For example, if something I have said reminded the client of his punitive mother, this will become a topic for discussion. If the client tells me he'd be more comfortable with a male therapist, I will make an appropriate referral.

At the start of the second session, I ask the client whether he's had any questions, reflections, or concerns arising from the initial session.

Should a client ask me a personal question unrelated to therapy, I will most likely gently reply that the question is not relevant to the therapy work we will be doing. For example, I will not answer a question such as, "Are you in a relationship?" or "What is your political position?" However, I may enquire whether there is any particular reason the client asked that question and offer clarification if I believe it could have impact on their therapy. For example, if the client suggests he can't work with anyone who has a different political position from his own, this might reflect a problem to be taken up in therapy. Further discussion will likely be required, and this may end with a referral to another therapist. Another question might be, "Do you have children?" This question may be relevant to a person who wants to discuss problems with her children and wants to know whether I have the experience to understand her concerns. If this is the case, I will answer the client's question honestly.

At the end of the second or third session, I set clients a "homework" task: to identify changes they wish to see in themselves with the help of psychotherapy. (See Appendix II for the Goals for Change template and an example of listed goals.) I ask the client to create a rough draft at home of changes he would like to see in himself, which we then review during the following session to ensure the listed goals are realistic, clear, and appropriate for work in psychotherapy. For example, if one of a client's stated goals is "to be happy," I'd ask him to identify what specifically he would need to change in order to be happy. The client might then say he would like to improve his social confidence, play sports more often, and be more assertive with family members. These then become individual goals. The client then rates on a scale from 0–10 how close he is to attainment of each listed goal, with 10 representing full attainment. I explain that the rating gives us a reference point for the work of psychotherapy. We then rate these same goals every two to three months to assess therapy progress.

<u>Learnings</u>
- Remaining flexible during the initial assessment is desirable, even while employing a structured interview.
- While it may be helpful to offer positive reinforcement for some of the client's behaviours and responses, false flattery will not further the therapy process.
- Setting goals provides a baseline for the work of therapy. The client's periodic rating of the goals allows both the client and the therapist to assess improvement.

7.
Recurring Questions about the Therapy Process: How the Art of Psychotherapy suggests answers

There are many questions I ponder concerning the process of conducting psychotherapy—questions rarely answered in textbooks or in formal education and training. These questions are important for determining the optimal interventions for individual clients with unique problems in specific situations. Often, these questions don't have straightforward, unequivocal answers, and they can't be addressed in a scientific manner. Rather, they depend more on the complex understanding of the multifaceted individual human being, a pursuit that is more in the domain of the *art of psychotherapy* than in that of science. Despite my many years of practice, I continue to reflect on the following questions as I engage with my clients.

When is it helpful to focus on details of early personal history, as often happens in psychotherapy? Under what circumstances might it be advisable for the therapist to avoid insisting on a detailed exploration of painful early events?

A therapist must consider whether exploring early personal history could cause harm or fail to advance beneficial therapy, as shown in the following case study.

Case Study: Mrs. K.

Mrs. K. was repeatedly beaten by her father when she was a child. Over time, she came to understand his suffering. He had also repeatedly apologized to her for the beatings. His mother had died when he was four years old, and his father had whipped him daily and threatened to throw him out on the street if he didn't behave. Mrs. K. said she had discussed the details of this early abuse with her father, had completely forgiven him, and they now had a close, loving relationship.

She comes to therapy with excessive expectations of herself—never feeling she is "good enough." Although she acknowledges that her self-expectations could be related to the beatings her father administered every time she made the slightest mistake when she was a child, I decided that a detailed exploration of her childhood experiences with her dad could harm their current good relationship. I also believed such a focus would be unlikely to advance her therapy. Had she wanted to further explore these early troubles, we certainly would have done so. She did not. Instead, we worked with Cognitive Behavioural Therapy to help her recognize her many commendable qualities in the present and to modify her unreasonable expectations of herself.

Under what circumstances is it best for a client in his regular life to ask for help and to accept help when offered? When is it best to encourage the client to be self-reliant?

The answer depends on whether the person has legitimate needs he is genuinely unable to fulfill by himself, or whether over-dependence on others has impeded healthy functioning and growth. The following two case studies show both sides of the coin.

Case Study: Ms. W.

Ms. W., a 55-year-old woman, came with back injuries and pain she had sustained in a car accident. Her mother, who had lost both parents when she was 14 years old, had brought up Ms. W. to be resolutely independent to ensure she would be able to cope on her own in case she (the mother) died young. While the client had many offers of help after the onset of her back injury, she insisted on doing everything herself, including carrying heavy bags from the supermarket. On one occasion, she fell and reinjured her back. This time, she could barely walk but was still refusing her sister's offer to do her grocery shopping. Much of the therapy focused on reducing the shame and fear she felt in accepting help.

Case Study: Mr. S.

Mr. S., who suffers from migraines, moved from his parents' home into his own apartment at the age of 35. Because he let them know that cooking exacerbated the migraines, they delivered his meals on a daily basis and telephoned him several times a day. His migraines were worse when his parents were away. When he told them about the increased pain of migraines during their absence, they stopped taking vacations out of town. He felt guilty and ashamed of his utter reliance on them. In this particular case, the therapy addressed the client's excessive dependence on his parents, including his (realistic) fear that they wouldn't always be present to take care of his needs. Slowly, over the course of therapy, he began to take on responsibilities, including cooking his own meals. Occasionally, he even brought his parents a meal he had cooked.

Under what circumstances is it useful to challenge a client's erroneous view of herself or of a particular situation (as revealed by inconsistent statements she herself made)?

Before the therapist challenges a client's mistaken self-perception, a therapeutic alliance must be well established. A person's erroneous self-perception is likely to be a defence, camouflaging a truth which contributes to the problem for which the client seeks therapy. Most likely, the client is unaware of this self-deception. For example, a client might say (and herself believe), "I'm always helping others, but nobody helps me," but later narrates a story in which someone carried her suitcase for her onto the train and placed it in the upper cabin. In this case, the therapist may reasonably conclude that the client views herself as a victim but fails to take into account that others do help her.

The following case study provides an example of such a situation:

Case Study: Helen

> Helen suffered from back pain, but was ashamed for others to see her look in any way disabled. She described a situation to me in which someone offered her a seat, which she gracefully declined, saying she would prefer to stand. Later in the same session, she complained of the many situations in which people didn't take her back injury into consideration, and she was left to suffer.

When the therapist brings the truth to light, the client may initially feel uneasy. Nevertheless, such an intervention may contribute to resolving the problems for which the client has come to therapy. In such a case, the therapist would explore with the client the underlying problems driving her belief that she is the victim, when in fact she may be the perpetrator or, as in the above case, she may be too proud to accept help that is offered. Of course, should the client truly be a victim, therapy interventions would take a very different route.

When is it more helpful to normalize a client's feelings of discomfort rather than work to decrease the discomfort?

A client may believe there is something very wrong with him because he feels shy and uncomfortable when he first meets a group of people who already know each other. This belief that he is *abnormal* will likely increase his anxiety and, thereby, his discomfort. It can help to let the client know that most people feel at least a little uncomfortable in a new social situation, that this is perfectly *normal*, and does not, as such, require treatment. Perhaps the main treatment in this case is to help the person feel comfortable with some temporary discomfort.

How might the therapist determine whether a problem a client brings to therapy—for example, chronic pain—persists because it allows the person to evade a situation he finds aversive?

This is referred to as "secondary gain" because the presenting problem of pain provides a kind of "reward" or "gain" by sanctioning avoidance of an undesirable activity or situation. The reason for wanting to avoid the activity is the real problem to be addressed in therapy.

For example, a child may say he has a stomach ache that allows him to stay home from school on a day he has a test he fears failing. Thus, he is rewarded for having a stomach ache and learns (consciously or unconsciously) that pain allows him to avoid a situation he fears. In this situation, it is important for the parent to recognize that it is fear of failing a test (or not having studied for the test) that needs to be addressed, and not the alleged problem of a stomach ache.

Another example concerns a 22-year-old insecure singer who is being pressured by her parents to begin her career in opera. She then develops temporomandibular pain disorder, hindering her ability to sing, just when she is scheduled for her first audition. If the temporomandibular pain is a "cover" for anxiety, the therapist would focus on performance anxiety rather than on the pain.

Under what circumstances is a direct route the best strategy for resolving the client's problem versus a more indirect approach?

For example, in the following case study, interventions aimed directly at reducing anxiety were not successful until the underlying problem triggering anxiety was first addressed.

Case Study: Sandra
Sandra suffered from agoraphobia and, try as she might, she couldn't get herself out the door. Just when she would be ready to step out, she would

experience intense anxiety, sometimes leading to a panic attack. The more we worked on reducing her anxiety as she was about to go out the door, the more her anxiety increased. On examining the source of the anxiety, it turned out Sandra felt shame about how she looked and feared what people would think of her. Despite her stated wish to decrease anxiety, she feared that with anxiety diminished, she would be compelled to go out into the world. We then worked on building her self-confidence until, gradually, she was able to go out into the world without feeling anxious.

Should regular exercise always be encouraged as one means of improving mental health? When might it be best to help the client accept some exercise limitations?

A person with moderate back pain and depression who fears the pain will increase with any movement may avoid all forms of exercise. Because a lack of movement leads to deconditioning which in turn results in increased pain with any movement, a therapist might best suggest the client see a physiotherapist to advise on gentle exercise. This would prevent deconditioning and, at the same time, contribute to improved mental health.

Alternatively, in the case of a highly active person who refuses to stop jogging and lifting weights after a sudden onset of pain, therapy to help him accept activity limitations—at least temporarily—is likely to be optimal. Explaining the rationale for temporarily decreasing activity can increase compliance.

Is it ever helpful for a therapist to "self-disclose"?

Any self-disclosure by the therapist must serve the therapy process and the client's goals. There is no place in therapy for self-disclosure that serves only the therapist. For example, a thera-pist explains to clients that her menstrual cramps might distract her during the session. If the therapist feels her therapy skills might be compromised, she should reschedule the session. Although it may help the therapist to excuse herself for anticipated distraction, it is not helpful for clients to expect a substandard session.

<u>Learnings</u>
- Psychotherapy interventions do not follow a straight, linear algorithm.
- The therapist must use keen judgement linked to her under-standing of the individual client and presenting problem(s) when formulating therapy interventions.
- Any self-disclosure on the part of the therapist must serve the goals of therapy.

8.

Common Factors in Successful Therapy

Research findings show no fundamental differences in effectiveness among the major psychotherapy approaches. Rather, certain "common factors" such as, for example, therapeutic alliance, account for a larger proportion of clients' improvement than do the elements of the therapeutic model itself, regardless of the model employed. Many years ago, Rozenzweig (1936) coined the term "dodo-bird hypothesis" to indicate that no particular psychotherapy method is superior to any others (Duncan, 2002).

Research on "common factors" examines the core active ingredients in effective psychotherapy across different theoretical models. In 1979, Jerome Frank popularized the idea of "active ingredients" that contribute to effective psychotherapy across diverse psychotherapy approaches. According to Frank, the essential ingredients of effective psychotherapy—independent of theoretical model used—include: an emotionally charged confiding relationship with a helping person, a healing setting, a rationale, and a conceptual scheme that plausibly explains the patient's symptoms. He also prescribed a ritual or procedure for resolving the patient's problems that requires the active participation of both patient and therapist, and which is believed by both to be the means of restoring the patient's mental health.

In a 2015 update on the subject, Wampold identified the common factors across theoretical models shown to be critical for effective psychotherapy outcome. These include: therapeutic alliance, a therapist's empathy, the creation of hope, and cultural adaptation (an approach that fits with the patient's beliefs, usually embedded in the culture).

In particular, evidence shows that therapeutic alliance is the best predictor of successful therapy outcome across theoretical models (Martin et al., 2000). Borodin (1979) described therapeutic alliance as a collaborative creation by the patient and therapist that includes shared goals, accepted recognition of each person's tasks within the relationship, and an attachment bond based on reciprocal positive feelings. Also important for therapeutic alliance is the therapist's demonstration of empathy, caring, a non-judgmental attitude, and interest in the patient's concerns. It can take several sessions for therapeutic alliance to be established, and it may take even longer for clients whose trust has been betrayed in the past.

The personal characteristics of the therapist have also been shown to significantly affect therapy outcome, especially in regard to establishing a therapeutic alliance with the client (Messer & Wampold, 2002). In one review, therapists able to form a positive alliance with their clients showed characteristics and behaviours described as "flexible, warm, alert, respectful, honest, trustworthy, confident, friendly, and open" (Ackerman & Hilsenroth, 2003).

The following case study illustrates the importance of therapeutic alliance, and the result of my failure to properly established it.

Case Study: Jeremy

Jeremy's first two sessions did not go well. In the first session, as I listened to him describe his problems, I observed a certain tension in his body and facial expression. When I asked him to tell me what he liked about himself, he replied that he was open, easy, and flexible. I gently pointed out a seeming contradiction between his self-description and the tense, taut, closed person I saw before me.

It was far too early to challenge Jeremy's view of himself. What I said felt confrontational and threatening to him. It raised his defences and created distance—hardly a recipe for promoting therapeutic alliance.

He replied that he was not usually tense, and that what I observed simply reflected his current situation: his girlfriend had recently left him and he was also experiencing writer's block together with a fear that he would never be able to write again.

Unfortunately, I didn't learn from the first session. The following week, Jeremy walked into my office, body tense and rigid. His manner of speech seemed excessively precise, and his face lacked expression. After a long silence, he reported he was feeling even worse than in the previous session. I suggested to him that both his relationship problems and his recent writer's block may have arisen from a pervasive tension he carried. My aim was to identify what I saw as the primary problem to be addressed in therapy. Again, he balked and strongly disagreed, insisting he was generally a relaxed, laid-back, and easy-going person.

As he left, I realized he and I were arguing about the core of his identity as a "laid-back guy," a self-perception he was far from ready to abandon. I had stepped hard on his toes and almost knocked him over instead of gracefully inviting him into the therapy "dance".

In the third session, he brought some poems he had written, hoping they would help me better understand him. The stakes at this point were high. I would have to find a way to connect with Jeremy, to show I understood him and that I was in step *with* him in the collaborative "dance" of psychotherapy.

I invited him to read a couple of his poems. In one poem, a feeling of sadness and despair was prominent. Instead of telling him this (and risking another disagreement), I asked what inspired him to write the poem. As we talked, he told me he had made a couple of failed attempts to publish his poetry. I asked whether the writing block he was experiencing might represent a fear of failing. He absolutely denied such a possibility. Not wanting to raise his defences again, I didn't argue. He explained that after his girlfriend had left him, he lost the spark that ignited his writing. He also mentioned that he had lost all desire to do other things he usually enjoyed.

While it was clear he was describing depression, I did not say so at this time. I only listened and acknowledged what he said. I let him lead, following the rhythm and direction of his "dance steps." One of his poems made me laugh. He smiled. I saw him soften and relax a little. In this third session, I was finally making use of "art," shifting from an approach that had created distance to one that allowed him to open up and engage with me in his therapy.

To make this shift—which finally succeeded in initiating therapeutic alliance—I had to reflect on the mistakes I had made in the first couple of sessions. I had to listen to him more closely and remove the judgment that had led to my earlier counterproductive interventions.

I now spoke to him about the sadness and loneliness reflected in some of his poems. He responded with tears and acknowledged the pain he had been feeling. I had finally gained his trust. A couple of months later, I was able to gently raise the issues I had misguidedly broached in the first couple of sessions when he wasn't yet ready. He now accepted that his social discomfort and tension had interfered with relationships, both male and female. The therapy ended a year and a half later. He was engaged to be married and wrote me a beautiful poem of thanks.

This example demonstrates my failed strategy at the start of Jeremy's therapy. I challenged his view of himself—his already-shaky identity—far too early. Such a destabilizing intervention should come only after trust and therapeutic alliance are well established. Knowing the optimal timing to confront or question a client's view involves *art*, especially when it concerns an entrenched belief pertaining to self-image. There are no rules, no theories, and no techniques to guide the way. Only a sensitivity to the client's "dance" movements can guide you. This case of Jeremy also demonstrates the need for the therapist to be alert to the client's reactions and to be open and flexible. If the first strategy fails to produce therapeutic results, the discerning therapist will be ready to alter course.

Learnings:
- Maintain flexibility.
- Determine optimal timing for interventions.
- Beware of triggering defences.

9.

Overcoming Clients' Defences

Defences can arise when a person feels emotionally threatened. In a therapy setting, a client who feels defensive may avoid revealing essential truths about himself to the therapist. As a result, progress in therapy is impeded or delayed.

To avoid triggering defences, the therapist must be sensitively attuned to the client's readiness to hear, process, and address a problem about himself of which he may not be aware, or whose presence he may not wish to acknowledge. If the therapist believes an intervention with a confrontational element will promote therapy, choice of words, timing, and tone of delivery require careful calibration.

As an example, you might wish to point out to an anxious client that, despite her agreeable demeanour, you are aware of an underlying anger. Rather than saying, "Although you seem to be extremely pleasant, you're really very angry," it may be more fruitful to say something along the following lines: "As you talk to me here, I see a kind, pleasant, calm person, but from a couple of things you've said, I'm wondering whether there might also be some anger, which you work hard to hold back. Does this feel about right, or is there something I've misunderstood?"

The first statement is phrased in a definitive, closed manner, which could easily be heard as a challenge and trigger defensiveness. The second open phrasing offers space for the client to disagree and to feel included in a collaborative process. No guideline for such a distinction can be found in textbooks, nor is the phrasing amenable to a formulaic strategy. Regardless of theoretical approach, a therapist's attentiveness, openness and flexibility enhance the therapy process.

The importance of being aware of a client's potential defences and the benefit of taking the time to explore a concern at the client's own pace became evident when I began to work with Derek.

Case Study: Derek

Derek, a pleasant, single, 38-year-old man reported severe ongoing pain in the groin area. Because tests ordered by his doctor failed to show any medical cause to explain the pain, I suspected the pain he described could be serving a psychological need to avoid sexual contact. Why this might be, I did not yet know. I didn't doubt that he felt some level of pain; rather, I thought it might feel more intense and disabling because it served a psychological purpose of which he was unaware. A couple of sessions in, I learned that a girlfriend had left him a couple of years earlier because a painful infection in the groin area at the time had temporarily impeded his sexual function.

Over time in therapy, it became clear that Derek was terrified of another failed sexual encounter, with the accompanying "pain" of shame and humiliation. I speculated that, in some sense, the continued focus on physical pain was easier for him to bear than the idea of being inadequate sexually. Sadly, his feeling of groin pain was not only keeping him from dating, but also from participating in athletic activities he had always enjoyed. He was sad and lonely.

I was keenly aware I would have to wait for some time, and obtain more information before confronting Derek with the psychological relief the groin pain may have come to serve. To deny him his groin pain too early in treatment would only increase his distress without being helpful.

In the fourth therapy session, he told me with great pride that he had saved a child from drowning the previous day. He was at the local beach when he saw a child in the water, clearly in trouble, about 20 metres away. Without hesitating, he ran into the water and swam at break-neck speed, catching the child just as she was about to go down again. He held her while swimming back to shore, where she was quickly attended to by a nurse who did CPR.

"How did you feel after you did that?" I asked. "You must have been exhausted."

"I felt terrific," he replied, "and more energetic than I've felt in a long time."

I might have asked, "So, no pain?" While it did cross my mind to do so, I realized that such a suggestion coming from me at this time might threaten his continued (unconscious) need to maintain the pain for psychological reasons. I also did not wish to undermine his good feeling of the moment. I decided to wait until his therapy had further progressed. He might eventually come to understand on his own, or with just a little prodding from me, that despite pain, there was much he could still do and be proud of accomplishing. At this time, I simply lauded him for his bravery and for rescuing the child.

Two weeks later, he came to his appointment lamenting the limitations that pain imposed on his life. His friends had invited him to join them on a two-day hiking expedition. This was something he very much wanted to do, but he feared such an activity would increase the pain. He was crying. I asked him whether he'd recently engaged in any strenuous physical activity. In a moment, he recalled his rescue of the drowning child. He smiled, saying, "And my pain didn't even get worse."

Not wanting yet to minimize his experience of pain, I explained how a surge of adrenalin can override pain, and I gave him several examples. I added that the same thing can happen when a person is fully engaged in an enjoyable activity. I hoped this explanation would encourage him to participate in activities with friends.

Because we had not yet discussed his intense fear and avoidance of a sexual encounter, I did not at this time raise my belief that pain, an acceptable rationale for avoiding sex, also allowed him to avoid feeling shame. Such an intervention would require still more time. Much more important now was that he could feel free to go hiking with his friends, which he did.

After about two months of weekly sessions, he acknowledged he was scared he would never be able to have an erection again. For this reason, he had recently turned down the advances of a girl he would have wanted to date. He said nothing about the pain. Nor was there any need for me to bring it up because he was back to most activities with his friends and had not been complaining of pain. I asked him to see his doctor just to make sure there wasn't a medical cause for erectile dysfunction.

He returned a couple of weeks later to tell me that tests ordered by his doctor had come back negative and that his doctor had mentioned that his feeling of pain was likely a substitute for a psychological problem. He seemed prepared to consider this possibility.

In the next session, he came in proudly saying he had been with a girl he liked and had "performed splendidly." At the end of this session, he asked shyly, "Do you think my worries about sex could have somehow created my pain?"

I asked him, "Do you have any thoughts about that?"

He did. He had come to the conclusion that the anxiety about his sexual performance had somehow caused the pain.

I responded, "Maybe, to some extent, but not entirely. It did start with an infection. What's most important is that you're without pain now and back to living your life fully and with enjoyment."

Derek's case shows how important it can be for the psychologist to recognize a defence, and to tread lightly in order to facilitate the client's eventual openness.

Learnings:

- To bring a defence to a client's awareness requires optimal timing.
- Pain (or other disability) can sometimes be a defence serving a psychological purpose.
- It is critical for a therapist to avoid concluding that pain serves a psychological purpose in the absence of clear evidence for such a conclusion.

10.

The Importance of Effective Communication in Therapy

Effective communication plays a key role in the art of psychotherapy. Knowing your client deeply includes understanding how best to communicate with her in a way that is readily comprehensible, using language familiar to her. This does not mean talking down to your client. Rather, the use of straightforward, everyday, nontechnical language will allow your client to comprehend what you say. Avoid medical jargon unless you have reason to believe it will be familiar to your client.

At the same time, an explanation of a technical term or diagnosis may in some cases, be appreciated. For example, some clients are eager to understand the physiological reactions associated with a panic attack. They then appreciate learning about sympathetic and parasympathetic arousal if these terms are explained clearly and simply, perhaps with an accompanying example. Similarly, answering a client's questions in a clear and respectful manner creates a collaborative climate that fosters therapeutic alliance. Avoid using a belittling and alienating response such as, "It's too complicated for you to understand."

Your choice of words matters. The following example demonstrates how use of technical language can lead to misunderstanding and misery in a client who is already suffering from pain.

Case Study: Richard

Richard, a 28-year-old man I saw at the multidisciplinary pain clinic, suffered from intense back pain. What upset him most was that he couldn't play hockey, his favourite sport. The pain clinic physician referred him for a consult with a neurologist. When I saw him three weeks later for a follow-up visit, he came into my office looking distressed—much more so than at his first appointment with me.

He sat down and immediately blurted out, "The neurologist said my pain is ridiculous."

He then told me that since his visit with the neurologist, he had spent most of his time at home in bed rather than going to work. He was feeling deeply ashamed to think he was making such a big fuss about a "ridiculous" pain. He began to sob.

I could not imagine the neurologist would have used the word "ridiculous" to describe Richard's pain, especially directly to his face. When I called the neurologist for clarification, I learned he had said to Richard, "Your pain is *radicular*." Of course, this was a word unfamiliar to Richard, who heard it as "ridiculous".

Had the neurologist said something like, "Your pain originates from the nerves in your spine," and perhaps added, "we call that 'radicular' pain," he might have spared Richard two weeks of misery over and above the back pain.

By contrast with the above example, a word or phrase can have a beneficial effect without the therapist's awareness or specific intent. In one case, after a client described several misfortunes she had experienced in a short period of time, I said in simple acknowledgement, "And you're still standing."

The following week she told me how this simple statement had helped her feel strong and capable in the face of difficulties. I had had no idea how therapeutic those few words had been.

Body Language and Tone of Voice

Body language, tone of voice, and facial expression provide vital sources of communication between therapist and client.

I have witnessed interns sitting in front of a client, leaning back with arms crossed, posture communicating aloofness and distance. A simple, relaxed placement of the arms, together with a slight forward lean towards the client, creates a sense of openness and caring.

Similarly, the client's body language offers a wealth of information. Is the posture rigid? Is he looking out the window rather than at the therapist? Are her hands tightly clasped? Is she fidgeting and constantly shifting in the chair? Is his face devoid of expression, or does his expression seem at odds with the words he speaks?

I refer to tone of voice as the "music" that accompanies the words. Some people may yell while saying, "I'm perfectly calm," or "I'm not at all angry." The "music" will often tell you more about the client's true feelings than will the words. Is there a certain sarcasm or derision in the tone? Or perhaps the client is speaking in a monotone and robotically reporting on a frightening situation without genuine engagement.

In much the same way, your tone of voice may influence the impact your words make. A couple of clients have told me that previous therapists had mouthed certain words they believed the therapist said to all clients just to make them feel good. Most important is not what you *intend* to communicate, but what the client hears and understands—what you *succeed* in communicating.

It's also possible that you are attentive and doing your best to communicate effectively while the client hears you through a filter of previous disappointments or betrayals. While different people may understand the same statement differently, in the end, it is your job to ensure that your message is received as you intend. This may require different wording and manner of delivery for different individuals.

For example, supposing a client tells you he got 90% on an exam, and you respond in a joking way, "You didn't do too badly, did you?" In this case you're acknowledging that he did really well. It's obviously important that you know your client sufficiently well to be confident he will receive your response in the positive manner you intend.

Feedback: Let Your Clients Know You Have Heard Them

The fact that you feel empathy or truly understand your client's distress is not sufficient. To create therapeutic alliance, you must communicate that you have heard and understood what a client has told you. You must convey your understanding with appropriate words, tone of voice, body language, and facial expression. Otherwise, a client can't know whether or not you are attending to, and understanding their story.

"Active listening" entails a brief response, facial expression, or reaction to the client's narrative. Reflecting back to the client by repeating his words is one of the common techniques used to demonstrate *active listening*. When employed judiciously and sparingly, this method can be useful. However, if it is repeated too often in a session, it is likely to lose its effectiveness and become no more than a vacuous echo of the client's words. This can be very annoying to the client.

As I was observing one intern conducting an assessment interview, I heard the client say to her, "Why do you keep repeating everything I say?"

Use of Imagery

The use of a well-chosen metaphor or other imagery can enhance the impact of your intervention (see Appendix III for examples). For instance, a therapist might say, "You are making every attempt to hold back your anger, but beneath your calm words I'm aware of a raging fire." The image of a "raging fire" is likely to create a stronger impression than simply saying, "It's clear you are angry."

In a different situation, to promote a healthier and more constructive behaviour or way of thinking, you might say to your client, "It may be hard to get rid of old habits—even though they are doing you harm—and replace them with new behaviours you're not accustomed to. This might feel much like trading an old, comfortable, threadbare coat for a brand-new coat that feels stiff and unfamiliar."

Sometimes, when I suggest a new, more constructive behaviour or thought process, a client who has heard the familiar "old coat" metaphor will smile and say, "But I like my *old coat*."

Listening Beyond the Words

A client you've seen a couple of times talks about recent difficulties. While you attend to his narrative, listen also beneath and beyond the words he speaks. The specific problems as presented by your client, including the piecemeal day-to-day challenges, are most likely only examples of the core problem or problems that have brought him to therapy. Listen carefully for underlying themes and repeating patterns to be explored. While sometimes a client will find the resolution of a specific situation helpful, addressing underlying maladaptive patterns is likely to be more helpful overall. The following case studies illustrate how important it is to look beyond the specifics of what the client is saying.

Case Study: Melinda

Melinda, a young woman with low self-esteem, felt insecure with her partner. From all the evidence she provided, it seemed that he loved her very much. When he came home late from work two days in a row, she accused him of seeing another woman. No matter how much he tried to reassure her about his need to finish a project at work, she refused to believe him. They began to argue intensely, leading her to threaten to leave the relationship.

She told me he was probably going to leave her and that by leaving him, she would pre-empt his exit. We could have changed the process to couple therapy in order to include him and try to resolve the problem between them. However, I was confident this was not a couple problem, but rather an example of her belief she was not good enough for him, as she had repeatedly insinuated. The difficulty arose from her low self-esteem. This was the problem to address in her therapy, with the goal of helping her to improve her self-esteem and confidence, rather than focus on the detailed, day-to-day problems between her and her boyfriend.

Case Study: Jane and Ken

Jane and Ken came to couple therapy because they repeatedly argued. Ken was well organized, goal oriented, and controlling, while Jane tended to be spontaneous, a little chaotic, and disorganized. On different occasions, Ken asked her to come to bed at a regular time, be ready to eat dinner at 6:00 p.m., follow directions for driving to a given destination, put her clothes away rather than throw them on the floor, and keep the volume of her music low before bedtime. Jane sometimes agreed to his wishes, but didn't always follow through. When she did comply, she became surly and resentful. At one session, Ken complained about the mess she had left in the bathroom after a shower.

We could have discussed strategies for motivating her to pick up her clothes from the bathroom floor after her shower in order to solve this specific problem, but other problems arising from their considerable differences would most likely have persisted. Discussing the dynamics between the two—his tendency to be controlling and her feelings of resentment when he insisted she do something he wanted her to do—were more likely to lead to general improvement in their relationship. As well, a discussion of their differences—his highly organized manner and her tendency in the opposite direction—perhaps concluding with a plan for him to become more generally tolerant and for her to become more mindful of the mess she leaves and how it upsets Ken, would likely be useful. After establishing these basic principles, a plan would be made for Jane to pick up after herself and for Ken perhaps to give her a hug when she does so, as reinforcement.

In conclusion, it is more beneficial for the therapist to address underlying themes and patterns that lead to repeated problems than to focus on resolving specific problems.

Learnings:
- Both the wording and the tone of a communication must ensure the client understands the message as the therapist intends.
- Use language the client understands; avoid jargon.
- Vivid imagery can enhance the impact of an intervention.
- Focus interventions on repeated *patterns* that trigger problems the client brings to therapy, rather than on the details of the individual problems.

11.
Can Psychotherapy Cause Harm?

The Hippocratic Oath, "First, Do No Harm," is a central imperative of medical practice. While this dictate is also key for conducting psychotherapy, psychologists are not required to make such a pledge.

While in most jurisdictions there is an organization to receive clients' complaints, there is no formal organization to oversee or monitor psychological treatments for lack of benefit or potential harm (Dimidjian & Hollon, 2010).

Harm can result from a therapist's inappropriate or unethical behaviour. The following example demonstrates how such behaviour can compromise a client-therapist relationship and, in the end, harm the client.

Case Study: Jennifer
Jennifer told me in her first session about a problem she had experienced with her previous therapist. Towards the end of one of her sessions, the therapist invited Jennifer to have coffee with her in a coffee shop, saying this would give them more time to discuss her problems in a relaxed setting. Jennifer happily agreed. Soon after she

and the therapist sat down at the coffee shop, the therapist began to tell Jennifer about other clients' problems. She added that she found some clients difficult to deal with because they were not compliant as Jennifer was. Jennifer began to feel uncomfortable and told the therapist she did not think it was right for her to know about the therapist's other clients. At this point, the therapist looked at her watch, said she had another appointment, quickly got up, put a five-dollar bill on the table, and departed. This left Jennifer gobsmacked. When Jennifer later called to schedule her next appointment, the therapist told her they were "not a good match" and terminated Jennifer's therapy.

The above example shows how a therapist's behaviour might be in egregious violation of ethics. Such situations, though rare, do occur.

Harm can arise when a client's situation is explained by the therapist's preferred theoretical model, despite absence of actual evidence for such an interpretation. In one example, the therapist explained to a 23-year-old client that her persisting anxiety originated in her mother's emotional abuse of her when she was growing up. While initially the client did not remember any such abuse, the therapist convinced her that the abuse had been so painful, she had repressed it. Before long, the client came to believe that. during childhood, she had been emotionally abused by her mother, which caused a serious rift between the two in the present. The harm arising from this situation affected not only the client, but also her mother who was seriously troubled by her daughter's anger with her.

Up to 10% of therapies may cause the client some form of harm (Lilienfeld, 2007). These are the reported numbers. Most likely, there are many more unreported therapies that cause some harm or provide minimal or no benefit. Harm can include exacerbation of symptoms, appearance of new symptoms, or over-dependence on continuous treatment. As well, a lack of benefit can be indirectly harmful when prolonged ineffective therapy dissuades a person from seeking help with a different psychologist whose treatment could provide more benefit.

Sometimes, during crisis counselling, patients are asked to re-experience in the *"here and now"* emotions evoked by the trauma itself, a process which may worsen symptoms and exacerbate distress rather than promote healing. Such treatments that focus on the experience or release of powerful emotions (catharsis) can help some clients, but may do harm to others (Samoilov & Goldfried, 2000).

It is essential for psychologists to monitor their own behaviour to ensure they abide by all the rules of ethics and avoid causing harm to their clients.

Learnings:
- First, cause no harm.
- The therapist must maintain a professional distance in the client-therapist relationship.
- Harm can arise when a client's problem is interpreted by means of a particular theoretical approach, in the absence of supporting evidence for such an interpretation.
- Avoid prolonging non-beneficial therapy.

12.
Theoretical Approaches in Psychotherapy

While a therapist's favourite theoretical approach may benefit some clients, it will not be helpful to all. In conjunction with *the art of psychotherapy,* a therapist would select the approach most likely to confer benefit to the specific client with a specific problem or problems in a particular socio-cultural context. The optimal approach is best determined after the initial assessment is completed. Of course, selection of the approach most likely to help requires knowledge of a variety of theoretical models.

A brief summary follows of prominent theoretical approaches currently employed in the practice of psychotherapy.

Cognitive Behavioural Therapy (CBT)

CBT, a pragmatic and relatively short-term therapy, arose in part as a reaction to the prolonged psychoanalytic approach that delved into early developmental history and emphasized unobservable concepts such as repression and the unconscious.

Cognitive behavioural therapy (CBT) employs variables that can be observed, operationalized, and measured, thus allowing for research, statistical analysis, and publication. By contrast, other currently employed therapy models are less amenable to similarly objective and quantitative study. For these reasons, CBT has become a primary contemporary approach for conducting psychotherapy.

In essence, CBT is based on the assumption that mental health is determined by what we *think* (cognition) and how well we *function* (behaviour). Thus, helping clients to think "correctly"—i.e., to change supposedly "distorted" thoughts into "accurate" ones—is assumed to improve mental health and general functioning. While this approach appeals to logic and shows benefit in many published studies, the basic tenets of CBT have been questioned (Lai et al., 2012).

Initially, CBT completely excluded affect (the experience of feeling or emotion) as a variable. In the past couple of decades, the important role of emotions has been integrated by some practitioners of CBT who have suggested that "emotional activation has the potential for improving the long-term effectiveness of CBT interventions" (Samoilov & Goldfried, 2000, p. 373).

Those who view affect as preceding cognition question the view that cognition is the driver of emotion, or that changing the client's thinking in a positive direction will reduce the painful feelings for which she seeks help. The debate concerning the primacy of affect over cognition (and vice-versa) continues. Storbeck and Clore, in their article on the interdependence of cognition and emotion, suggest that "affect is a potential moderator of all kinds of cognitive operations, from perception and attention to implicit learning and implicit associations" (2007, p. 1215).

When a person who has become disabled after sustaining an injury in a car accident says, "I am totally useless," a CBT therapist might challenge this thought by pointing out the many things the person is still able to do despite the presence of limitations, thereby suggesting he is not "totally" useless.

While pointing out that the person is not completely useless may help to some extent in some instances, the therapist might also address the client's intended meaning: "I'm totally useless" expresses the client's *feeling* of being useless. The therapist needs to respond to the client's despondent emotion, resulting from loss of function, as opposed to singularly focusing on an allegedly distorted thought. If the therapist understands the client's intended communication, the stated thought is not distorted; rather, it is an expression of emotion.

Cognitive emotional behaviour therapy (CEBT) has been developed more recently to incorporate emotion into the CBT model. Even so, the negative impact on emotions when the therapist alleges a client's thoughts are distorted persists within CEBT (Corstorphine, 2006).

APET Model

According to the APET model, emotions precede thoughts, thereby influencing cognitions and perceptions. The letters, *A*, *P*, *E*, and *T* represent sequentially: **A**ctivating agent, **P**attern matching, **E**motion, and **T**hought. The model allows for therapist flexibility to intervene at any of these four stages, in the order most likely to be helpful to the individual client.

The following example can be understood within the framework of the APET model: A woman who was beaten by her father (*Activating agent*) may attribute violence to men in general (*Pattern matching*), which then may evoke the *Emotion* of fear of men with the *Thought* that men are violent.

The activating agent is the triggering stimulus. Pattern matching is a form of classical conditioning whereby a present situation or stimulus triggers a negative emotion much like one formerly experienced in a similar situation. For example, pattern matching may describe a circumstance in which a passenger who has been in a major car accident (activating agent) experiences dread (emotion) when passing the same location in the future (pattern matching). In another example, a smell often evokes an emotional memory from the past.

The primacy of emotions reflects brain activity in the limbic system and the amygdala, the oldest brain structures concerned with survival. The pattern matching process is an instinctive part of human brain functioning, especially when the stimulus is one that causes significant emotional arousal. In such circumstances, according to Joseph LeDoux (2018), activity in the amygdala (emotional brain) precedes responses in the neocortex (cognitive brain). Thus, the action in the emotional brain comes first and then influences cognitions and perceptions.

Psychodynamic Approach

There are several psychodynamic models derived from Freud's initial psychoanalytic theory. In general, pathological emotions, thoughts, and behaviours in adulthood are understood to arise from unconscious processes whose origins lie in an individual's early experiences. Sometimes these are assumed to present themselves in symbolic form. For example, in dream analysis, guns, snakes, or anything that is longer than it is wide may be understood to be phallic symbols with sexual or male-related implications.

Psychodynamic therapies aim to help the client recognize how past experiences continue to wield influence in the present. For example, someone whose mother punished her severely if she talked back when she was a child may, in adulthood, have difficulty being assertive. As a result, others often take advantage of her. Once she comes to recognize the root of her failure to assert herself, the therapist will try to help her understand that she is now a competent, independent adult and no longer the helpless child her mother controlled.

Humanist-Existential Approaches

Humanistic and existential therapies share a belief that humans can make responsible choices in order to create and enhance meaning in their lives. These ideas form the basis for conceptualizing the client's problems, establishing therapeutic goals, and deciding on therapy interventions. As well, both approaches focus on the individual client as a whole person rather than as only a collection of pathological symptoms. Humanistic-existential therapies emphasize—to varying degrees—acceptance of a situation or condition one cannot change, responsibility for things one can change, and a drive to fulfill personal potential.

To help clients find meaning in their lives, existential therapists encourage their clients to make authentic and responsible choices in the face of anxiety-provoking conditions such as isolation, loneliness, despair, and losses—including death of loved ones or the anticipation of their own finitude.

My work with Stephen, as seen in the following case study, is an example of the use of the humanist-existential approach, which I believed would work best for this client.

Case Study: Stephen

Stephen, a 37-year-old artist, who often exhibited his paintings, had succeeded in selling several of them. Nevertheless, he was not at all confident in his talent as an artist. He had been referred to psychotherapy after his doctor diagnosed him with high blood pressure and severe anxiety.

Stephen had inherited a substantial amount of money from his parents and had no need to work for a living. This led him to feel guilty. He displayed compulsive behaviour. Stephen lived with a supportive wife and two children, aged four and seven. He felt compelled to vacuum the house on a daily basis, tidy the mess he insisted he made with his painting, cook dinner every evening for the family, bring the seven-year-old to and from school, and also help him with his daily homework. He would not allow his wife to attend to any of these chores. She had given up trying to get him to relax and to spend more time on his painting.

When I asked Stephen what he enjoyed doing, he told me that painting was his favourite activity but that he rarely had time for it. He also told me that he experienced great pride and satisfaction each time he sold a painting. He hoped that therapy would help him find more time for his painting. This then became the primary goal of therapy.

It was no simple task. We worked together to alleviate his guilt, reduce his compulsiveness, and shift some of the household chores to his wife. As well, he was gradually able to acknowledge that his painting was not an indulgence and that he could regard it as his life's *work*.

After 6 months of therapy, Stephen was surprised to find he had more time to paint and that it gave him great joy and fulfillment. Apart from selling two more paintings, he was giving them as gifts to family members and friends, all of whom were delighted to receive them. His anxiety had decreased, and with deep breathing techniques and daily walks, Stephen's blood pressure had come down.

Biopsychosocial Model

The biopsychosocial model, first introduced by George Engel in 1977, emphasizes the interconnection among psychological, social, and biological factors as contributors to both illness and health.

For example, a woman comes to therapy suffering from anxiety and low self-esteem. She was raised by a highly anxious father and a critical mother. She was bullied at school. Now, as an adult, she believes that no matter how hard she tries, she is never "good enough."

She may have inherited a low threshold for sympathetic arousal from her anxious father and been made to feel inadequate by her critical mother as well as by the classmates who bullied her when she was a child. These situations have led her to experience pervasive anxiety and feelings of unworthiness. The feelings of anxiety and never being "good enough" reinforce and exacerbate each other. Thus, the biological (genetic), social (experiences with mother and peers), and cognitive (belief she is inferior) act in concert rather than as independent influences.

In this situation, a therapist who uses the biopsychosocial model may recommend medication and introduce relaxation strategies to reduce anxiety (sympathetic arousal). Interventions are also likely to include emotional and cognitive work to help her recognize her strengths and understand and feel that she is no longer a helpless child.

The *biopsychosocial model*, with its emphasis on interrelated psychotherapy approaches, is in some sense a precursor of integrative psychotherapy.

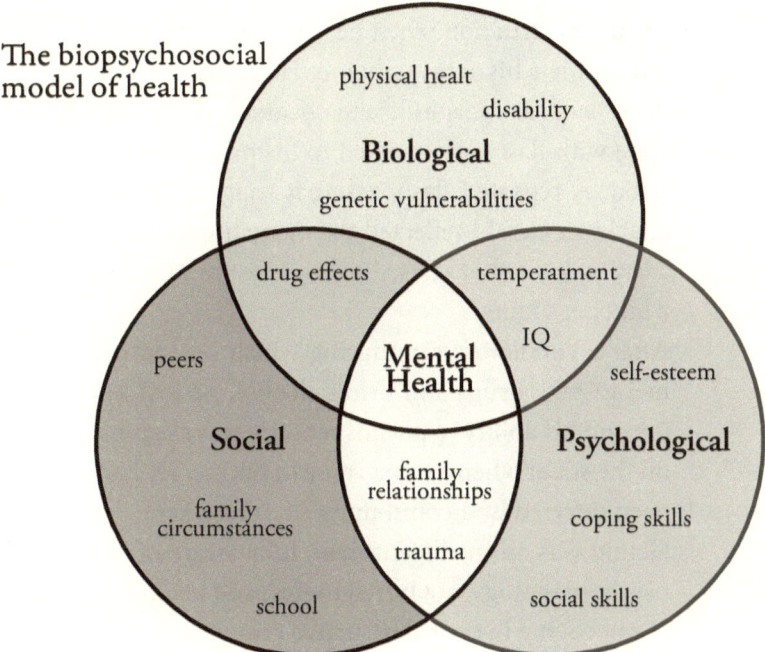

The biopsychosocial model of health

PhysioPedia online (2016)

Integrative Psychotherapy

A single theory approach to psychotherapy becomes a mould into which the client, the problem(s), and the treatment interventions must be forced to fit.

The integrative psychotherapy model offers the therapist a wide range of theoretical approaches and techniques to select from, with integration of the selected elements most likely to help the individual in therapy (Zarbo et al., 2016). An example of this model is illustrated by the case of Gerald.

Case Study: Gerald
Gerald had been severely abused by his single father, both emotionally and physically. He got a

job in construction when he was seventeen years old and left his father's home. He began to take drugs such as morphine and cocaine to help him cope with flashbacks related to his painful childhood. A repeated flashback that triggered panic attacks in Gerald reflected the many times he ran away as his father chased him while brandishing a butcher's knife.

After a couple of years during which he continued to take drugs and drink alcohol, he lost his job and his ability to pay his rent. He was sleeping on the street when he first came to see me. He had been referred by a community social worker.

Gerald was an intelligent man, fully aware of his psychopathology, but he felt useless and incapable of improving his self-destructive lifestyle.

We worked with a combination of psychoanalysis to help him address his painful childhood experiences, and cognitive behavioural therapy to reinforce his positive qualities and skills until he was able to view himself as a competent, worthwhile individual. He spent 3 months in a drug rehabilitation facility while continuing his psychotherapy with me on a biweekly basis. Eventually, he was able to get a job as a cleaner in a hospital setting, and move into a basement studio apartment.

Using the humanistic-existential model, we discussed Gerald's need to feel useful and valued. He started doing volunteer work at the hospital, spending time speaking with isolated geriatric patients. Doing something for others helped him feel useful and valued. Eventually, he overcame his feelings of being a burden, which he had carried since childhood. Thus, Gerald was able to become a well-functioning, healthy individual and to feel good about himself as a result of therapy that combined the use of several different theoretical models.

A psychologist with experience in—and the inclination to apply—the art of psychotherapy will make use of integrative psychotherapy, applying carefully selected elements from a combination of models designed to promote the well-being of a unique person with a problem or problems in a particular sociocultural context. Such therapy requires the psychologist to be knowledgeable in a broad range of psychotherapy models and to apply imagination, flexibility, and a deep understanding of the individual seeking help.

To clarify the elements of integrative psychotherapy, Brooks-Harris (2008) laid out the dominant theoretical approaches used in this model, together with the primary variables each addresses, as shown in the following chart.

Theoretical Approaches	Focal Dimensions
Behavioral	Actions
Biopsychosocial	Biology
Cognitive	Thoughts
Experiential	Feelings

Multicultural	Cultural Contexts
Psychodynamic	Interpersonal Patterns
Systemic	Social Systems

Learnings
- There are several different therapeutic models currently employed in psychotherapy.
- The therapist's favourite model may not benefit all clients.
- The therapist with knowledge of several theoretical approaches is best positioned to select an optimal therapeutic strategy for a given person with a problem or problems, arising in a particular sociocultural context.
- The *Integrative model* comes closest to employing the art of psychotherapy by allowing the therapist to select elements from different models that are most likely to be of benefit to a particular client.

13.
The Effective Clinical Psychologist:
A Summary

The effective clinical psychologist comes to the psychotherapy encounter with proper training, knowledge of the science of psychotherapy practice, and the skills to apply therapeutic artistry.

Their scientific knowledge will include familiarity with the different therapeutic models, information about—and ability to apply—protocols and techniques appropriate for the problems different clients present, and awareness of the relevant evidence in the published literature.

The art of psychotherapy takes the therapist beyond the science to an in-depth understanding of the multilayered person in treatment, including cultural background and personal history. Other elements reflecting professional artistry include sensitivity to the dynamics of the relationship with the client, the ability to create therapeutic alliance, and a sensitivity to the client's emotional vulnerabilities. As well, in working with clients, the therapist displays empathy, warmth, a non-judgmental attitude, and an ability to encourage realistic hope. These characteristics have been shown to promote positive therapy outcome (Elliott et al., 2018).

The art of psychotherapy also involves a general openness and flexibility, the capacity to anticipate the client's reactions to interventions, and the ability to intuit optimal timing for a given intervention. All this comes with an in-depth understanding of the many-sided individual client.

For therapists who have the skill and inclination, use of appropriate humour at the appropriate time may promote the client's engagement, thus facilitating therapeutic alliance. As well, use of metaphor or cultural references familiar to the client may enhance the impact of an intervention.

In summary, psychotherapy that integrates a felicitous blend of science and art to match the individual client's needs and circumstances has been shown to ease distress and improve well-being (DeAngelis, 2019). Science provides the underpinnings, while art frees the therapist to minister to the unique client with a specific personal, social, and cultural history.

At the same time, the psychologist who treats clients with certain disorders (e.g., panic disorder) or who works with special populations (such as autistic individuals) may need to more strictly apply standardized, evidence-based techniques.

APPENDIX I
Psychological Assessment Report
(with Fictional Example)

Patient's Name: Judith Smith

Brief Description and Reason for Seeking Therapy: Intelligent, insightful, 40-year-old married woman with severe anxiety and panic attacks; suffers from emotional abuse by husband.

Developmental History: Ms. Smith reports she was severely neglected and physically abused by her parents when she was growing up. When she was only six years old, both parents often went out in the evening after she was put to bed, despite her terror of being left alone. Starting at age seven, her father hit her with the strap if she cried, talked back to him, or failed to complete a task perfectly. She was bullied at school from kindergarten to grade three, after which the bullying stopped and she began to be included with a group of friends. She does not know what triggered the positive change. When she was eight-years old, her parents began to fight. Her father often slapped her mother in the face while her mother tended to be helpless and passive. Ms. Smith reports that both parents had a drinking problem. Her mother died when Judith was nine years old, and she went to live with her maternal grandparents, who were kind and loving. An older sister has been diagnosed with schizophrenia. Ms. Smith has a close relationship with her brother (one year younger), whom she regards as her best friend.

Current Family: Married for eight years (second marriage) to an emotionally abusive man who has drug addiction problems. Her seven-year-old daughter is healthy and seems to be doing well overall.

Mental Health: Pervasive anxiety, sometimes with panic attacks (since childhood). Occasional depressive episodes that can last up to one month. During depressive episodes, Ms. Smith also experiences periods of depersonalization.

Physical Health: No medical problems except back pain—sometimes disabling for days at a time.

Medications: Remeron 30 mg, Tylenol prn up to 3/day.

Work History: Has worked as an accountant's assistant for the past year. She has worked at a variety of other jobs, none lasting longer than two years.

Summary: Judith Smith comes to therapy for treatment of anxiety with panic attacks, as well as intermittent depression. Despite significant mental health problems, Ms. Smith shows resilience, intelligence, and good insight. Her life history is marked by ongoing physical and psychological abuse. Her childhood home environment was unstable, and she suffered from neglect. Her current (second) husband is emotionally abusive. She is highly motivated to improve her marital situation and her mental health.

APPENDIX II
Goals for Change (with Fictional Example)

What I Would Like to Change About Myself
0–10 scale; 10 = full attainment

Goals	Date: 11/24/22 Rating	Date: Rating
Decrease self-criticism	3	
Decrease perfectionism	4	
Decrease guilt	2	
eat more healthfully	3	
eat more regularly (3/day)	5	
Decrease need for control	3	
Increase assertiveness	6	

↑ self-esteem	3	
cope better with (extreme) emotions; ↑ emotional regulation	3	
↓ erroneous belief that people are angry with me	6	
↓ people-pleasing	3	
↓ cigarettes per day	5	
↓ time spent on social media	7	
↓ saying "sorry"	2	
↓ self-sabotaging behaviour	4	
accept others' imperfections	7	

APPENDIX III
Imagery to Promote Therapeutic Impact

Images and metaphors, such as the ones below, can
enhance the impact of interventions.

Dance of psychotherapy
Meaning/usage: You are "dancing" *with* a partner (client).
Sometimes you lead; sometimes your partner leads. You anticipate
the direction of your partner's moves. You are careful to avoid
stepping on your partner's feet.

*Sometimes, no matter how much we tend to an infested shrub
and spray insecticide on the leaves, it doesn't heal because it's the
roots or the soil that needs tending.*
Meaning/usage: Sometimes, the underlying cause of a symptom
has to be treated, not only the symptom. For example, when
a person has panic attacks, it's important to understand and
treat the root cause of the attacks, not only aim to get rid of the
panic attacks.

Pilot light is out; must find fuel to relight it.
Meaning/usage: For depression, lethargy, lack of motivation.

*Ingesting something rotten creates indigestion, which must be
processed to get it through and out.*

Meaning/usage: A poisonous thought someone has convinced the client to "swallow."

A person who won't take the life-saver ring thrown to him and drowns.
Meaning/usage: A client who insists on being independent, to his detriment; need to examine why self-sufficiency is so critical.

Black thing.
Meaning/usage: A physical feeling of dread or despair. A therapist creates a strong visualization of the "black thing"; then, with the client in a relaxed state, makes the "black thing" slowly fade, disperse, lighten (and maybe even disappear). Alternatively, the therapist could replace it with the image of a gradually brightening sunshine.

Each time the curtains close, you use your arm muscles to pull them open and let the light back in; your muscles gradually strengthen.
Meaning/usage: Development of resilience.

You keep digging yourself deeper and deeper into the same hole until you can't see out anymore, and you are blind to any other possibilities.

Meaning/usage: For someone who keeps repeating the same self-destructive pattern. The goal is to pull the person out of that "hole"—perhaps by fashioning steps for her to climb out and broaden her vista, so she can "see" other options.

If we can uproot the weeds that invade your garden, perhaps we'll make room for the flowers to grow.

Meaning/usage: To remove impediments blocking someone's strengths.

*You have worked very hard and made important changes, but
now you are stuck at the entrance of the bridge leading to your
desired destination, terrified to cross.*
Meaning/usage: Fear of taking the last step to achieving a goal.

*Rigid tree branches break in strong wind, whereas flexible
branches bend with the wind.*

Meaning/usage: For clients whose rigidity renders them vulner-
able to breaking down at the slightest adversity.

*A desirable behaviour or reaction is "on the menu" but not
"available in the restaurant right now."*
Meaning/usage: For a client who has displayed a functional
thought or behaviour at some point in the past but is not able
to do so now. The fact that it's "on the menu" demonstrates
that it is within the client's repertoire but needs encouragement
and strengthening.

Climbing a mountain to get to the other side.
Meaning/usage: Represents a strenuous effort to achieve a
desired goal.

*An old winter coat is threadbare and doesn't keep out the cold
anymore, but is familiar and feels comfortable. It's hard to give it
up in favour of a new coat that feels stiff and alien (but will keep
the person warm, as a coat should).*
Meaning/usage: To suggest changing a habitual self-sabotaging
behaviour for a new healthy one.

A raging fire within a client, but no equipment to douse it.
Meaning/usage: Uncontrolled anger or rage.

A balloon that flies too high, eventually bursts, and falls to the ground.
Meaning/usage: a client who becomes excessively excited upon formulating a new project and then plummets with despair when the idea doesn't pan out. Also to depict a client who displays a repeated pattern of ups and downs.

REFERENCES

Ackerman, S.J., and Hilsenroth, M.J. (2003). A review of therapist characteristics and techniques positively impacting the therapeutic alliance. *Clinical Psychology Review, 23*(1), 1–33.

Al-Din Rumi, J. (2008). The Guest House. *Academic Medicine, 83*(6), 588.

American Psychiatric Association. (2013). *Diagnostic and Statistical Manual of Mental Disorders* (5th ed.). https://doi.org/10.1176/appi.books.9780890425596

American Psychological Association. Division of Clinical Psychology. (n.d.). Clinical psychology: science and practice. Retrieved August 28, 2023, from https://www.apa.org/about/division/div12.

American Psychological Association. Division of Clinical Psychology. (n.d.). *Task Force on Promotion and Dissemination of Psychological Procedures: A Report Adopted by the Division 12 Board - October 1993*. Retrieved August 28, 2023.

English Standard Version Bible. (2001). ESV Online. https://esv. literalword.com/

Borodin, E.S. (1979). The generalizability of the psychoanalytic concept of the working alliance. *Psychotherapy: Theory, Research & Practice, 16*(3), 252–260.

Brooks-Harris J.E. (2007). *Integrative Multitheoretical Psychotherapy.* Lahaska Press.

Corstorphine, E. (2006). Cognitive-emotional-behavioural therapy for the eating disorders: working with beliefs about emotions. *European Eating Disorders Review, 14*(6), 448–461.

Curran, J., Parry, G.D., Hardy, G.E., Darling, J., Mason, A.M., & Chambers, E. (2019). How Does Therapy Harm? A Model of Adverse Process Using Task Analysis in the Meta-Synthesis of Service Users' Experience. *Frontiers in Psychology, 10*, 347.

David, D., Cristea, I., & Hofmann, S.G. (2018). Why cognitive behavioral therapy is the current gold standard of psychotherapy. *Frontiers in Psychiatry, 9.*

DeAngelis, T. (2019). Better relationships with patients lead to better outcomes. *Monitor on Psychology, 50*(10), 38.

Dimidjian, S., & Hollon, S.D. (2010). How would we know if psychotherapy were harmful? *The American Psychologist, 65*(1), 21–33.

Drescher, J. (2015). Queer diagnoses revisited: the past and future of homosexuality and gender diagnoses in DSM and ICD." *International Review of Psychiatry, 27*(5), 386–95.

Duncan, B.L. (2002). The legacy of Saul Rosenzweig: The profundity of the dodo bird. *Journal of Psychotherapy Integration, 12*(1), 32–57.

Fenn, K., & Byrne, M. (2013). The key principles of cognitive behavioural therapy. *InnovAiT, 6*(9), 579–585. https://doi.org/10.1177/1755738012471029.

Frank, J.D. (1974). *Persuasion and Healing: A Comparative Study of Psychotherapy* (Rev. ed.). Schocken Books.

Frank, J.D. (1979). Successful psychotherapy. *The Journal of Nervous and Mental Disease, 167*(5), 325–325.

Hofmann, S.G., & Weinberger, J.L. (2007). *The Art and Science of Psychotherapy*. Routledge.

Jay, M. Evan. (2023). Sigmund Freud. In *Encyclopedia Britannica*. Retrieved August 28, 2023, from https://www.britannica.com/biography/Sigmund-Freud

L'Institut national d'excellence en santé et en services sociaux. (2018, January). *Equitable access to the psychotherapy services in Quebec.* https://www.inesss.qc.ca/fileadmin/doc/INESSS/Rapports/ServicesSociaux/INESSS psychotherapy services EnglishSummary.pdf

Lai, V.T., Hagoort, P., & Casasanto, D. (2012). Affective primacy vs. cognitive primacy: Dissolving the debate. *Frontiers in Psychology, 3.*

LeDoux, J.E., & Hofmann, S.G. (2018). The subjective experience of emotion: a fearful view. *Current Opinion in Behavioral Sciences, 19,* 67–72. https://doi.org/10.1016/j.cobeha.2017.09.011

Lilienfeld, S.O. (2007). Psychological treatments that cause harm. *Perspectives on Psychological Science, 2*(1), 53–70.

Marchant, J. (2016). Cure: A journey into the science of mind over body. *Deutsche Zeitschrift Fuer Akupunktur, 59*(4), 54–54.

Martin, D.J., Garske, J.P., & Davis, M.K. (2000). Relation of the therapeutic alliance with outcome and other variables: A meta-analytic review. *Journal of Consulting and Clinical Psychology, 68*(3), 438–450.

McHenry, S. (2022). "Gay is Good": History of Homosexuality in the *DSM* and Modern Psychiatry. *American Journal of Psychiatry Residents' Journal, 18*(1), 4–5.

Messer, S.B., & Wampold, B.E. (2002). Let's face facts: Common factors are more potent than specific therapy ingredients. *Clinical Psychology: Science and Practice, 9*(1), 21–25.

Norcross, J.C. (1990). An eclectic definition of psychotherapy. In J.K. Zeig and W.M. Munion (Eds.), *What is psychotherapy? Contemporary Perspectives* (218–220). San Francisco, CA: Jossey-Bass. Cited in: American Psychological Association. (2012). *Recognition of Psychotherapy Effectiveness.*

Physiopedia contributors (2023, July 27). *Biopsychosocial Model.* Physiopedia. Retrieved August 28, 2023 from.

Reisner, A.D. (2005). The common factors, empirically validated treatments, and recovery models of therapeutic change. *The Psychological Record, 55*(3), 377–399.

Samoilov, A., & Goldfried, M.R. (2000). Role of emotion in cognitive-behavior therapy. *Clinical Psychology: Science and Practice, 7*(4), 374.

Storbeck, J., & Clore, G.L. (2007). On the interdependence of cognition and emotion. *Cognition and Emotion, 21*(6), 1212–1237.

Wampold, B.E., & Imel, Z.E. (2015). *The Great Psychotherapy Debate: The Evidence for What Makes Psychotherapy Work* (2nd ed.). Routledge.

Wolman, B.B. (1989). *Dictionary of Behavioral Science* (2nd ed.). Academic Press.

Young, C., & Heller, M. (2000). The scientific 'what!' of psychotherapy: Psychotherapy is a craft, not a science! *International Journal of Psychotherapy, 5*(2), 113–131.

Zarbo, C., Tasca, G.A., Cattafi, F., & Compare, A. (2016). Integrative Psychotherapy Works. *Frontiers in Psychology, 6*, 2021.